THE ROAD TO PARADISE

THE STORY OF THE REBIRTH OF THE STRASBURG RAIL ROAD

BY WILLIAM M. MOEDINGER

PUBLISHED BY THE STRASBURG RAIL ROAD SHOP, INC.
STRASBURG, PA

CREDITS

LEAVING PARADISE
William Moedinger

FRONT & BACK COVER: Strasburg Rail Road locomotive #90 heading westbound. Photo by David Boyer.

MAP BY: Brenda Ulmer

ACKNOWLEDGMENTS: The author expresses gratitude to the following persons whose unselfish assistance, particularly in the realm of photographs, made this book possible: John J. Bowman, John D. Denny, Jr., J. Huber Leath, Mrs. Helen H. Long, Jon W. Simpson, Lynford Swearer and Gordon Roth.

DEDICATION

1913 – 1992

TO MARIAN WEAVER MOEDINGER
WHOSE LONGTIME OFFICIAL INVOLVEMENT
IN THE AFFAIRS OF
THE STRASBURG RAIL ROAD
CONTRIBUTED SO MUCH TO ITS SUCCESS.

ACROSS THE FLATS
William Moedinger

STOCKHOLDERS SPECIA
William Moedinge

On Saturday, June 5, 1982, in recognition of the railroad's one hundred and fiftieth birthday, the Strasburg inaugurated a nine-day-long celebration by recreating a typical passenger train of the year 1959, when the reincarnated carrier brought back passenger travel over the four and one-half miles between Strasburg and Paradise. Reserved exclusively for stockholders of the Strasburg Rail Road Company, the first of the three trains operated that overcast June day is shown approaching Carpenters Crossing along the side of Cherry Hill. In a special timetable issued for the occasion, it was identified as train no. 2, "The Sesquicentennial." With a 10:00 AM departure time, it was scheduled back in East Strasburg at 10:45 so that those directors who chose to ride this train would have ample time to make their regular quarterly meeting at the company office at East Strasburg.

CARPENTERS CROSSING
William Moedinger

PREFACE

The Strasburg Rail Road is a venerable institution. Founded during the first term of President Andrew Jackson, it was incorporated by a special Act of the Pennsylvania Legislature that was signed into law by Governor George Wolf June 9, 1832. Precisely when the railroad first turned a wheel is still a matter of patient research, but the earliest timetable found to date indicates Strasburg trains were scheduled as of December 1851. It is safe to say, without the slightest fear of contradiction, that the railroad's trains are well into the second century as familiar facets of the eastern Lancaster County scene.

The railroad literally grew up with America, alternately prospering or eking out a precarious existence as dictated by the economic vicissitudes of the growing nation. The first major economic setback occurred around the turn of the century when a streetcar line was completed between Lancaster and Strasburg. With most of its passenger traffic diverted to the trolley, regular passenger trains were discontinued. While a daily mixed train continued to operate for years, passenger fares ceased to be an important item of income. Until the end of World War II, carload freight interchanged with the Pennsylvania Railroad kept the road solvent. Improved highway transport following the war increasingly diverted freight to the trucks so that by the mid-Fifties the Strasburg had become the equivalent of a red ink operation. Finally, in 1957, really hard times fell upon the struggling carrier. In addition to the woes of dwindling freight revenues and mounting operating costs, a series of storms of hurricane proportions literally wrecked the railroad by causing washouts and blowing huge trees across the tracks. So destructive had been the storms that an immediate embargo was placed on all incoming carload freight. Further deteriorating the road's almost untenable situation was the fact that it had by this time become part of an estate whose heirs viewed any expenditure toward rehabilitation of the railroad tantamount to throwing good money after bad. Consequently, petitions for abandonment were filed.

During those dark hours, while petitions for abandonment were being considered by Pennsylvania's Public Utility Commission and by the Interstate Commerce Commission in Washington, the late Henry K. Long, an industrialist and railfan from nearby Lancaster, was attempting to save the historic railroad. He was trying to organize a group of interested individuals who would purchase the property at scrap value and preserve and restore it by operating it as a hobby. Interest in the project was widespread until it was learned that a share of stock would have to sell for $450.00 (there were only fifty shares outstanding). At this juncture most of the prospective stockholders disappeared

with the speed of light. Undeterred, Long and three other railfans continued the campaign, buttonholing anyone who looked as though he could beg, borrow or steal the price of a share of stock. Progress continued painfully slow until someone hit upon the idea of making every stockholder a vice-president. The gimmick worked; and on November 1, 1958, acting as trustee for the purchasing group, Henry Long tendered a check in the amount of $18,000.00 to the Homsher Estate. The 126-year-old railroad faced life anew.

This book, in picture and prose, tells the story of the rebirth of the Strasburg Rail Road from the epochal day in late 1958. This is the sixth printing of the fourth edition of THE ROAD TO PARADISE. In order to incorporate all of the changes that have been made in the last twelve years since the publication of the third edition, there have been major revisions, particularly in the areas of photographs and captions. In order to further bring the reader up-to-date, new text matter has been added.

William Moedinger
Lancaster, Pennsylvania
July, 1995

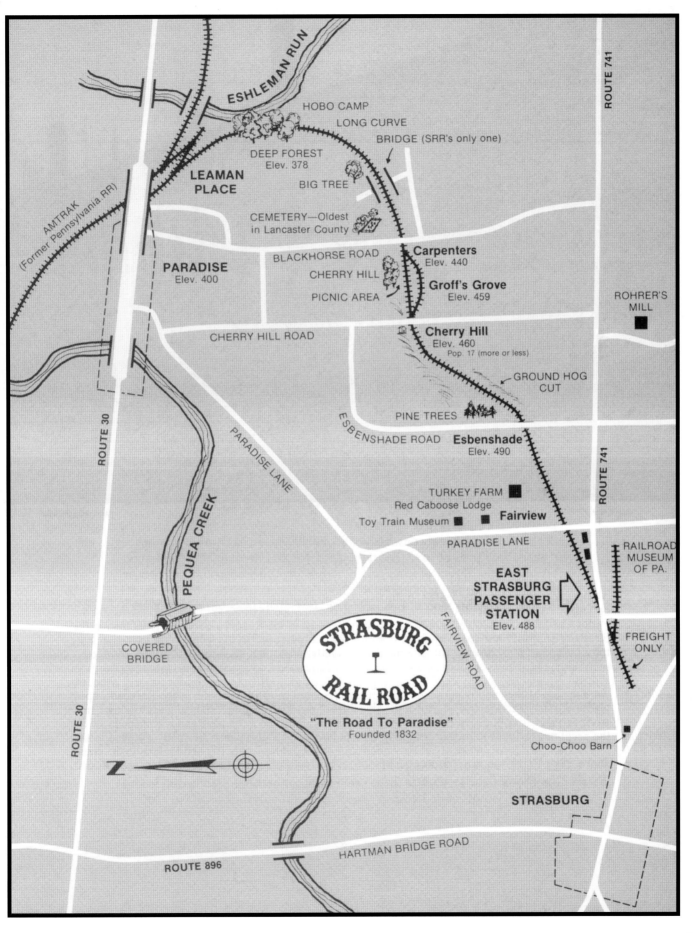

ESHLEMAN RUN

ROUTE 741

HOBO CAMP
LONG CURVE
BRIDGE (SRR's only one)

DEEP FOREST
Elev. 378

LEAMAN PLACE

BIG TREE

CEMETERY—Oldest
in Lancaster County

AMTRAK
(Former Pennsylvania.RR)

PARADISE
Elev. 400

BLACKHORSE ROAD
CHERRY HILL
PICNIC AREA

Carpenters
Elev. 440

Groff's Grove
Elev. 459

ROHRER'S MILL

CHERRY HILL ROAD

Cherry Hill
Elev. 460
Pop. 17 (more or less)

GROUND HOG CUT

ROUTE 30

ESBENSHADE ROAD

PINE TREES

Esbenshade
Elev. 490

ROUTE 741

PARADISE LANE

TURKEY FARM
Red Caboose Lodge
Toy Train Museum

Fairview

PEQUEA CREEK

PARADISE LANE

RAILROAD MUSEUM OF PA.

EAST STRASBURG PASSENGER STATION
Elev. 488

FAIRVIEW ROAD

FREIGHT ONLY

COVERED BRIDGE

STRASBURG RAIL ROAD

"The Road To Paradise"
Founded 1832

Choo-Choo Barn

ROUTE 30

N

STRASBURG

HARTMAN BRIDGE ROAD

ROUTE 896

PARLOR CAR MARIAN
William Moedinger

Among the twenty-four individuals who purchased the Strasburg Rail Road back in 1958, neither the most optimistic investor nor the most rabid railfan dared to imagine that anything as ornate and luxurious as the Parlor Car Marian would ever grace the passenger consist of the Road To Paradise. Even though the Strasburg's normal consist of turn-of-the-century open platform coaches has won it wide acclaim among those concerned with historical integrity, the Parlor Car Marian's ornate decor and luxurious accommodations surpass anything extant today in the United States. Researched, designed and built in the Strasburg car shops under the direction of Vice-President and Chief Mechanical Officer Linn W. Moedinger, it is the last word in turn-of-the-century passenger car opulence. Rebuilt in 1988 from one of the Railroad's open platform coaches. It is replete with all of the amenities of victorian elegance: stained glass windows, rare wood carvings, deep pile carpets, luxurious overstuffed furniture and a complete galley equipped with all the necessary facilities to prepare tempting repasts for the car's occupants. Normally assigned to the railroad's regular hourly trains, it is also available for private groups and catered functions. In the photo above, Santa Claus is shown boarding the Marian on one of the pre-Christmas Santa Claus specials that operate annually over the first two weekends in December.

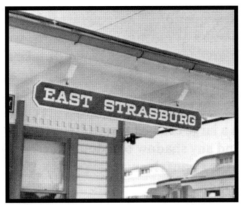

William Moedinger

DAWN OF A NEW DAY

Among some of the prospective shareholders who viewed the property in the summer of 1958 there was considerable confusion as to whether they would be investing in railroading or agriculture. In fact, one cautious would-be investor even went so far as to suggest that it might be prudent for someone in the organization to join the local chapter of the 4-H Club, just to be on the safe side. To be sure, at either end of the line ample evidence was clearly visible that the company was railroad oriented. This was particularly so at the Strasburg end. In the little brick engine house was a twenty-ton, gasoline-mechanical Plymouth locomotive purchased new from the manufacturer when the last steam locomotive was retired back in 1926. In the same building was the only operable piece of equipment owned by the railroad, a one cylinder Northwestern gasoline section car. Outside, with its worn wheels rusted to rails hidden beneath the tall grass, stood a weatherbeaten box car of unmistakable Pennsylvania Railroad ancestry. Stretching to Leaman Place, however, on what was supposedly a railroad right of way, was a four-and-one-half-mile swath of dense growth consisting of lush grasses and assorted other cover crops whose very luxuriance hinted at some of the most fertile soil in a county already famous for its productive farms.

The doubters and the querulous were assured that beneath the vegetation was four and one-half miles of railroad track of sorts, with a gauge of approximately four feet, eight and one-half inches, give or take an inch here and there. The railfan members of the group had actually made a trip to Leaman Place with the Northwestern motorcar. And while they hadn't ridden all of the way because the wooden ties and steel rails in places were buried in the mud, an occasional probing with a large crowbar inevitably resulted in the reassuring ring of steel on steel. Beyond any shadow of a doubt there was still a railroad which linked Strasburg with the Pennsylvania Railroad at Leaman Place. It was just a matter of uncovering it.

When enough interested people had been convinced that they would in fact be buying a railroad and not a four-and-one-half-mile-long grass patch, progress on the project moved into high gear. Although final settlement was still several months in the future, spokesmen for the owning estate saw no reason why the group shouldn't work on the railroad and its equipment, at its own risk, of course. The Plymouth locomotive, while mechanically sound, needed corrective work performed on it before the Interstate Commerce Commission would permit it to be operated. Since a railroad cannot function in the finest tradition without at least one locomotive, No. 1 was dispatched on a flatbed truck to the Reading Railway's shops in Reading, Pa., where its four wheels were ground down to the proper contour and other alterations and improvements made to conform with recent ICC directives.

In the meantime, in anticipation of the return of the Plymouth, the railfans, aided by sympathetic volunteers, descended on the right of way with everything from chain saws to power mowers in an all-out effort to dig out and clear the track to Leaman Place. President Henry Long came forth

with a huge wire brush affair driven by a diesel engine mounted on a four-wheel section car. Not only did it clear the track of weeds and brush, but it frequently removed whole ties in varying stages of decay, a circumstance the railroad could ill afford.

Before the first train could be run to Leaman Place, two major obstacles had to be overcome. A year earlier route 741 had been resurfaced, and the Homsher Estate had given the highway people permission to pave over the railroad crossing just east of town. There had been a verbal understanding that the highway department would remove the paving should the railroad find it necessary to run another train. Unfortunately, there had been a change of administration and in political circles the promises of one party are not binding upon the succeeding one. Consequently, the cost of opening the crossing fell upon the railroad. This entailed digging up the crossing, raising the rails to the level of the new paving, reballasting the raised track and repaving. The second obstacle, just east of where the present car shop stands, was a ten-foot stretch of track suspended in mid-air as the result of a washout. To correct this situation, ton after ton of crushed stone was dumped into the gaping hole until the track again rested on solid ground.

Resplendent in its new Royal Blue livery, No. 1 arrived back in Strasburg just in time to go to work. On November 8, to be exact, it made its first trip to Leaman Place Junction to pick up a box car spotted on the interchange track by the crew of the Pennsy's Saturday morning local freight. Pennsylvania box car No. 50065 will always remain prominent in the annals of the revived carrier. Loaded with company material, including splice bars, spikes and other items essential to track maintenance, it was the first car to be picked up and hauled to Strasburg

The Santa Claus Specials of the Strasburg Rail Road have become an annual event in the pre-Christmas social calendar of Lancaster County. They are at once the railroad's way of celebrating the return of passenger trains to Strasburg rails and a way of expressing its appreciation to the thousands of riders who are helping to make the railroad restoration possible. (Top photo) In full regalia, the crew of that first Santa Claus Special train in 1959 poses around Plymouth locomotive No. 1 at the Paradise end of the line. Shown, from left to right, are: Santa Claus (Les Myers); conductor Don Hallock, on the coach platform; fireman Ben Kline, on the engine steps; on the coach platform almost hidden by the engine cab, Linn Moedinger; leaning out of the cab window, engineer Bill Moedinger; and near the front of the engine, Winston Gottschalk. (Middle photo) In the center of the photo is the trolley that virtually put the Strasburg out of the passenger business back in 1901. The location is Elliott's Corners at the intersection of Route 222 and Penn Grant Road. At the time the author took this photo, trolley patronage had decreased to the point where the Strasburg car ran only between the junction and Strasburg. Passengers for Strasburg rode the Quarryville car as far as this point where they changed to the Strasburg car. These trolleys ceased operating Sunday, April 10, 1932, just two months short of the Strasburg Rail Road's 100th birthday. On the trolley timetable, this point was known as Beaver Valley Jct.

(Bottom photo) Lad George Arend was a familiar figure around the Strasburg Rail Road during the last thirteen summers of his life; for it was here he continued a career in railroading that began in 1900. During the 68 years prior to his coming to the Strasburg, Lad worked for twenty-one railroads in such varied occupations as brakeman, conductor, claims adjuster, auditor, ticket agent and detective. During his spare time, Lad built wooden models of many of the trains he had worked on. More than a dozen of these models are on display in the Rail Road Shop. Known to many folks as "Mr. Railroad," Lad was killed in an automobile accident on July 8, 1982, in his hometown of Franklin, Ohio, when he drove his red sports car through a stop sign and was struck by another car. Lad George Arend was 97 years of age.

L. Swearer

William Moedinger

LAD AREND

since the embargo on carload freight was lifted. Three days later, on the following Tuesday evening, No. 1 made its first trip to pick up a car-load of revenue freight, Chesapeake and Ohio box car 283970, loaded with grain for the rail-road's one and only customer, the mill at Strasburg. Everyone chipped in that evening to fill the Plymouth's gasoline tank.

On November 1 Henry Long had presented a check in the amount of $18,000.00 to the lawyers for the Homsher Estate. The railroad was now under new management. The railroad was ours. On December 30 the local freight again placed a car on the interchange track, but unlike the previous two, this one was a passenger coach. Reading Railway coach number 90849 it was, and those of us who made the trip that evening were every bit as happy as when we received our first electric train as children. In fact, we actually made a second trip that evening just for the sheer fun of it. Five days later, on the following Sunday afternoon, the railroad went back into the passenger business. At 1:30 on January 4, 1959, from the mill siding along route 896, conductor Hallock gave the highball (the starting signal in railroad terminology) for the first passenger train departure in approximately forty years. Two trips were scheduled that afternoon and both departed SRO. "The Road To Paradise" was born.

The running of those two passenger trains was more than a mere historical event. To the dedicated men who gave so freely of their time and talents to save America's oldest short line rail-road from abandonment, it signaled the dawn of a new day.

Income during those first few months of the experiment was pitifully meager, contingent on erratic freight revenues and passenger fares gleaned from the two Sunday-only passenger trains. At times there was scarcely enough money in the till to refuel No. 1's fifty-gallon gasoline tank. More than once the men pooled pocket resources in order to buy enough fuel to make a freight run. The $4,500.00 paid-in surplus had gone into repairing the Plymouth locomotive, opening the grade crossing with route 741 and filling in the washout.

Freight revenues from the very beginning fell way short of expectations. Passenger revenues, on the other hand, more than made up for the disappointing carload revenue. As the season progressed the Sunday-only schedule was expanded to include Saturday afternoon runs, as well as a thrice-weekly evening trip during the summer months. After an eight-month trial the road's directors voted unanimously to pursue the passenger business on a larger scale. Here, it was obvious, was where the money was; and money, great gobs of it, was what the railroad needed most. The expense of running a railroad, even a microscopic one such as the Strasburg, is almost beyond the average layman's imagining. Yet, for the first time since the new owners took over less than a year earlier, income was beginning to show at least some signs of catching up with expenses. To develop and pursue the program, management was authorized to borrow, that is, if a bank could be found whose directors hadn't seen the railroad firsthand. The local bank had seen it and wanted no part of it.

Finally, an area bank was found that agreed to extend the railroad a modest line of credit, and the Strasburg embarked upon a program of restoring the railroad to that of a typical steam short line around the turn of the century. One of the first items on the agenda was that of acquiring a medium-size steam locomotive to replace the Plymouth. Acquisition of land east of the town of Strasburg for terminal facilities and parking was an important part of the program.

ALL PHOTOGRAPHS – John Denney, Jr.

The Strasburg Rail Road re-entered the passenger business January 4, 1959. (Top two photos) The left one shows the train arriving back in Strasburg after the first trip; while the right photo depicts the switching operation at Leaman Place. It was a unique operation, for there was no passing track. Upon arriving at Leaman Place, the passenger car was pushed onto the slightly inclined interchange track with the Pennsylvania Railroad. In this photo, the passenger car is being uncoupled from the Plymouth, which will back away and into the clear. Then the passenger coach brakes will be released and the car will coast past the Plymouth to the end of track at Leaman Place. (Bottom photo) Later in the same year, a two-car train passes what is now the railroad's East Strasburg terminal. The coach immediately in back of the Plymouth is former Maryland & Pennsylvania coach No. 20 which starred in the M.G.M. film RAINTREE COUNTY. It is now Strasburg coach WILLOW BROOK, named for the John R. Groff farm through which the railroad passes at Cherry Hill. The second coach, formerly Reading Company No. 90849, is now Strasburg's CHERRY HILL.

To justify the expenditures required to acquire the above items, it would be necessary for the railroad to haul a greater volume of passengers, but to haul more people would require additional passenger coaches; so the railfan members of the group scoured the Northeast for appropriate coaches. Early in 1960, land was acquired and construction commenced on what is now the railroad's East Strasburg terminus. The Strasburg's first steam locomotive, Canadian National number 7312, was purchased, moved to Strasburg and became our number 31. Don Hallock discovered several ancient coaches rotting away on remote sidings in New Hampshire. These were purchased at scrap value and moved here for restoration. Finally, a beautiful little Victorian station, built in 1882, was purchased, cut into nine sections for transport and reassembled at its present location. With all the paper work completed, the final segment of the railroad's passenger program fell into place when the ICC permitted the 31 to be fired up in time for Labor Day weekend. ∎

William Moedinger

Very early and late in the season, when steam trains operate only on weekends, daily passenger service is provided with motor car No. 10, originally built in 1915 for the narrow gauge Lancaster, Oxford & Southern Railroad. In the photo, No. 10 is shown crossing the Strasburg's only bridge.

(Top photo) For a time the reactivated Strasburg used the Homsher Mill's freight siding along route 896 to load and unload passengers. As the number of riders increased, pedestrian and vehicular congestion increased accordingly, so that the railroad decided to build a new terminal two blocks east along route 741.

(Middle photo) Originally built in 1882 twenty miles from its present location, the East Petersburg station was moved in nine sections reassembled where it now stands and renamed East Strasburg under the direction of Donald E. L. Hallock. It is a perfect example of the Victorian elegance of those early times.

(Bottom photo) This privy-like edifice was the reactivated railroad's first passenger depot. Surrounded by an open-air waiting room amid the clutter of the Homsher mill's lumber yard, it was scarcely comparable with New York's Grand Central Terminal in its more spacious days; but it did eliminate the necessity for collecting fares on the train.

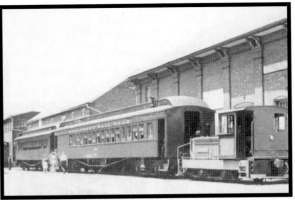

John Denney, Jr.

L. Swearer

L. Swearer

THE JOHN BULL REPLICA
William Moedinger

Unlike the internal combustion engine, which requires little more than the flick of a switch to set it into motion, the steam locomotive requires considerable coaxing and encouragement before it will tackle the day's chores. Once these conditions have been met and the locomotive emerges with a full head of steam, it stands ready to take on virtually any assignment, with a display of steam, steel and sounds that has captivated mankind since steam propulsion became part of the railroad economy. Shown arriving in Leaman Place on its first full-length trip over the Road To Paradise under its own power, the John Bull Replica seems to bear out that phenomenon. As part of the two-day Pennsylvania Railroad Locomotive Spectacular sponsored jointly by the Railroad Museum of Pennsylvania and the Strasburg Rail Road, the John Bull Replica arrived in Leaman Place just in time to touch pilots with Pennsylvania's No. 1223 as Amtrak's Eastbound Broadway Limited, right on the advertised, barreled through town.

William Moedinger

ALL STEAMED UP

If ever anyone compiles the annals of the Strasburg Rail Road from the very day of its founding back in 1832, the return of steam on the Labor Day weekend in 1960 must stand out as the high noon of all events in that historical documentation. It was a glorious occasion; and, as one who actively participated in it, I am sure that it will remain forever in my repertoire of things remembered. Thirty-four years had elapsed since the last steam locomotive chuffed between Strasburg and Paradise, but none ever chuffed by more grandly. No. 31 was more than equal to the occasion; and the immaculate appearance of both engine and tender bespoke the long hours of affectionate grooming by its proud crew.

In those thirty-four years many changes had taken place. The wooden water tank at Leaman Place had long since disappeared. Facilities for loading coal into the tender were non-existent. The brick enginehouse, which formerly housed the road's steam locomotives, had been altered through the years and would not accommodate the 31; only No. 1 could squeeze through its constricted portals.

Steam presented many immediate problems; and improvisation was the order of the day in order to coal, water and service the fifty-two-year-old Baldwin. Of these many problems, one was becoming increasingly serious; and that was what No. 31 was doing to Strasburg track. Her 26-ton axle loading, aided and abetted by thirty years of deferred maintenance by the previous owners, nearly caused a halt to all steam operations. As soon as that 78-ton ex-Canadian National 0-6-0 began pounding the track, rails began to spread on curves, others were broken wherever a combination of poor alignment and rotted ties coexisted, and ties under rail joints were literally driven into the soft ground after a summer shower. So urgent was the need for a complete track overhaul that virtually all other plans and programs were immediately shelved so available funds could be funneled into track upgrading.

All summer long a three-man crew had worked on weekends and evenings installing second-hand ties, replacing missing spikes, tamping low spots and reinforcing the one bridge in anticipation of steam. In just three weeks after 31 went into service, the track, or what passed for track, was a shambles. Tangents had been transformed into zigzags; curves, into kinks. In just three weeks these men learned the fundamentals of railroad track construction and maintenance. They learned that the rigid wheelbase steam locomotive, particularly one such as No. 31 without either lead or trailing truck, requires a considerably higher standard of track construction than the more flexible gasoline or diesel engine. They also learned that track is the basic ingredient in an operable railroad and that it should be constructed and maintained properly or not at all. New ties, heavier rail and splice bars, and a foundation of stone ballast were ordered for the patient.

Broken rails or no, the steam locomotive was here to stay, at least as far as Strasburg directors were concerned. Revenues had literally zoomed with the revival of steam; and only steam, they reasoned, could begin to attract enough revenue to pay for the track renewal. People came from far and near to ride behind steam again. With only three coaches and a bench-fitted gondola available, the road's two cabooses were added to the consist.

Because existing facilities did not permit steam operation during the months of freezing temperatures, No. 31's boiler was drained and all pipes blown out with compressed air as cold weather approached; and No. 1, the old reliable Plymouth, took over. Obviously, people who vis-

ited the railroad after No. 31 had been retired for the winter were disappointed. One querulous young mother who brought her flock for a train ride after 31 had been retired for the winter did concede that it would be pretty expensive to fill that huge boiler with anti-freeze.

In spite of the strain on the road's finances caused by the enforced track program, plans were approved for a new enginehouse east of the depot. Three months and $12,000 later the structure was completed. Two tracks wide and 140 feet long, it provided, among other things, a track pit so essential to the proper servicing and maintenance of steam motive power.

With steam here to stay and passenger trains already exceeding the rated capacity of the twenty-ton Plymouth during the peak of the tourist season, it seemed prudent to cast about for additional steam locomotives of the size and weight compatible with the Strasburg operation. Authorization was granted by the Directors so that today, either through purchase or lease, the Strasburg Rail Road has the finest stable of operable steam power in the United States. Four are owned; two are leased. Of the six, all are operable except number 4. The remaining five are assigned to the road's passenger trains.

No. 31, Strasburg's first steam locomotive, as stated earlier, is without lead or trailing truck and is much harder on track than any of the other engines, which all have leading trucks. Boilerwise and mechanically, it is in excellent condition. It is maintained in operable condition for standby service, for it has sufficient tractive effort to handle any passenger consist the railroad now operates or contemplates operating in the foreseeable future.

No. 4, the second steam locomotive purchased by the Strasburg Rail Road, though inoperable

(Top photo) With a reduced post-season consist of four coaches, No. 31 approaches Carpenters crossing on the westbound run to East Strasburg. The light colored cars, just back from location along the Hudson River, were used in the filming of the 20th Century Fox production HELLO DOLLY back in the late sixties. Notice the shocked corn, a sight peculiar to the Amish country where harvesting is done very much like it was a century ago.

(Second photo) Although No. 31 is not a passenger locomotive, it performs well at any task assigned it; and it has no problem handling an eight-car passenger train. No. 31 pulls a great deal of the freight moved over the Strasburg. In the second photo from the top it is shown approaching the Stoltzfus lane with three cars of plastic pellets and former Pennsylvania GG1 No. 4859 which was the first GG1 to pass Leaman Place back on Saturday, January 15, 1938. Ultimately, engines like the 4859 replaced steam east of Harrisburg on the Pennsylvania; but here we see the electric moving behind steam on one of its last moves before being put on display.

(Third photo) No. 4, America's last operating camelback, is shown here pulling a seven-day train up to the 1.2% grade between Cherry Hill and Esbenshade crossing. Invisible, however, is Strasburg's diesel No. 33 providing a great deal of the muscle to get the heavy train up the grade. No. 4 had the power to do the job, but it did not have sufficient steaming capacity. No. 4's life on the Strasburg was very short for this reason. During those few short years, the little camelback proved to be a great attraction, especially for those people who lived in the anthracite region where cab-astride-the boiler engines had been a common sight years earlier.

(Bottom photo) In this photo of No. 4, the camelback is shown passing the Esbenshade turkey farm on an overcast, cold day. Eastbound, moving a seven-car train was no problem, because the grade, for the most part is down.

John Denney, Jr.

John Denney, Jr.

John Bowman

John Bowman

today, is maintained for display and may be seen at the East Strasburg terminal. Built by the Baldwin Locomotive Works in 1902, this diminutive 0-4-0, as No. 1187, performed switching chores for the Reading Company for forty-three years, until the railroad sold it to a steel plant in Birdsboro, Pa. At the Birdsboro plant of the Colorado Fuel & Iron Company, the engine became No. 4. Seventeen years later, in 1962, Strasburg purchased the No. 4.

No. 4, thus far, is the only steam locomotive to arrive under its own power. Although the engine soon turned out to be too light for the Strasburg's growing passenger traffic; during its operating days on the Strasburg, America's last operating Camelback turned out to be a charmer, captivating the attentions of railfans and tourists alike with its melodious and throaty stack music and its cab-astride-the-boiler configuration. Unlike most steam locomotives, whose cabs are hung on the rear of the firebox, the Camelback's cab was forward of the firebox and hung across the boiler. Almost exclusively, the camelback configuration was a feature prevailing on those eastern railroads that burned anthracite coal, which required a much larger firebox (grate area) to produce the necessary heat to turn water to steam. In later years, locomotive designers found ways of hanging the cab on the rear of these large fireboxes.

Often called the Mother Hubbard type, the last Camelback locomotives were retired in the mid-fifties. To the author's knowledge, only two remain today: Former Central Railroad Of New Jersey No. 592 is preserved at the B. & O. Museum in Baltimore, while former Reading Company 1187 is on display on the mall at East Strasburg, Pa.

Considerable mystery surrounds Strasburg steam power during the 126 years before the present owners purchased the property. There is absolutely no record of a steam locomotive being purchased new from the builder. All, presumably, were hand-me-downs from the mighty Pennsylvania. A number of them were of the 4-4-0 wheel arrangement similar to No. 1223, which the Strasburg began leasing from the Pennsylvania Railroad in the mid-sixties. Now the property of the Railroad Museum Of Pennsylvania, the Strasburg continues to lease it; for it is a perfect match for the Strasburg's carefully restored turn-of-the-century open platform coaches. Coupled to the head end of four or five of these coaches, the 1223, resplendent in its gold trim, is the very epitome of mass transport during the golden age of steam.

In 1968, the Strasburg purchased Baldwin-built No. 90 from the Great Western Railway of northeastern Colorado. Outshopped in 1924, it is an out-and-out freight locomotive whose first forty years were spent trundling long, heavy trains of sugar beets to the company's towering mill in Loveland, Colo. It is of the 2-0-0 wheel arrangement known as a Decapod, and is the last of that type operating in the United States today. Its presence on the Strasburg serves to exemplify the independent and nonconformist spirit of the typical American short line railroad. Only a short line would have the audacity to assign an engine such as No. 90 to a passenger train.

In 1972, the Strasburg purchased No. 89, a 2-6-0, from the Green Mountain Railroad. Known as a Mogul type, it is an example of light steam power suitable for use in both freight and passenger service. Before being purchased by the Green Mountain, it belonged to the Canadian National Railway from whom the Strasburg purchased its No. 31.

As soon as the Strasburg had consummated the purchase of Green Mountain's No. 89 in the late

(Top photo) In the Strasburg Rail Road's stable of iron horses, the 1223 is the most photographed. It is the classic example of the AMERICAN type locomotive which was so prominent during the great years of railroading in this country. During its long career on the Pennsylvania Railroad as well as the Strasburg Rail Road it has been featured in many motion pictures and TV programs. In the top scene No. 1223 is shown during the taping of the BALLAD OF THE IRON HORSE at Esbenshade crossing.

(Second photo) Uncluttered with the many appliances so common to latter day steam locomotives, the 1223 had the clean lines of the early speedsters that plied the nation's railroads around the turn of the century. In its day, the American type locomotive was an all purpose engine that moved passenger and freight trains on both the large and small railroads. In this scene, the 1223 and its train has just come off Long Curve and is crossing the Strasburg's only bridge, which spans the lane into an Amish farm.

(Third photo) The 1223 is also the pride and joy to those who manage and work on the Strasburg Rail Road. Occasionally, on the occasion of one of the railroad's quarterly director meetings at which property inspection is a prime object, the 1223 is enlisted to pull the director's special train. The scene opposite shows the special director train on June 3, 1972, with engineer Benjamin Kline, Jr. awaiting clearance to make the run back to East Strasburg. The location is Leaman Place and the car behind the engine is the president's private car STRASBURG.

(Bottom photo) The Strasburg Rail Road's largest locomotive is No. 90, purchased from Colorado's Great Western Railway when that railroad turned to diesel power many years ago. It is an out and out freight locomotive, so it has plenty of power to handle anything the Strasburg assigns to it. It normally pulls the railroad's hourly trains which are too heavy for the 1223. In the opposite photo it is shown about to run around its train at Leaman Place many years ago just as Penn Central's PENNSYLVANIA LIMITED barrels by en route from Chicago to New York with GG1 4929 on point.

ALL PHOTOGRAPHS – William Moedinger

spring of 1972, its immediate concern was to move the sixty-two-year-old 2-6-0 from the seller's roundhouse in Bellows Falls, Vermont, to its own shops at East Strasburg with a minimum of delay. Accordingly, the most direct route was selected and No. 89 was prepared for the 555-mile journey. When all had been made ready, employee Linn Moedinger was driven to Bellows Falls with instructions to ride 89's cab all of the way through to home rails.

Participating carriers gave engine and rider preferential scheduling on regular time freights; and by the evening of the third day engine messenger and his charge had reached Penn Central's Buttonwood Yard in Wilkes-Barre, Pa., which left only 165 miles to go to home rails at Leaman Place Junction. Here, along the rapidly rising waters of the Susquehanna River, disquieting rumors about an impending flood were rampant. Rumor suddenly became reality when Penn Central ordered all railroad personnel to vacate the railroad yard with instructions to seek higher ground. Tropical storm Agnes was about to make itself felt.

Reluctantly, Linn gathered up his possibles, abandoned engine and retreated to the second floor of a vacated firehouse across the street where he hoped to keep an eye on his charge. During the ensuing night, he could hear the wall of water roaring down the valley; and, at daybreak the following morning, he looked out upon a vast lake where only the previous evening had been a sprawling railroad yard. No. 89 was nowhere to be seen; it was completely submerged. Not even its tall smoke stack was visible; during the night, the flood waters of the Susquehanna River had risen to the second floor of the abandoned firehouse. Later that day, Linn was rescued from the second floor of the firehouse by two men in a rowboat.

With virtually all communications between Wilkes-Barre and the outside world cut, Linn took refuge in the high school where the Red Cross had set up quarters for those who had been driven out of their homes by the rising waters. The high water was slow to recede, and it was days before Linn could get back to his engine and assess the damage. During the rising waters, virtually all freight cars in the yard that night had floated off their trucks. As the waters receded, they were deposited in all sorts of crazy positions around the huge freight yards. Except for being caked with mud, No. 89 and its tender saw little damage. It was many days before an engine could venture into the yards to rescue the engine and tender. The contemplated seven-day journey between Bellows Falls and East Strasburg emerged as a twenty-seven-day adventure for engine and engine messenger.

In 1983, the Strasburg acquired former Pennsylvania Railroad No. 7002, one of that road's famous fleet of high-wheeled 4-4-2 Atlantic types, of which there were more than 600 at one time. Representative of a class of steam locomotives that began to emerge from the erecting shops during the closing year of the nineteenth century, these were the locomotives that ushered in the Golden Age of railroading, when speed and on-time performance were the hallmark of travel on the Standard Railroad Of The World, as well as every other first class carrier of the day. Before the era of steel passenger cars and the Pacific and Hudson types, engines like the 7002 were able to take over from the Americans, like the 1223, when train lengths began to exceed the pulling capacity of the 4-4-0's. Even after the advent of steel passenger cars, and the heavier and more powerful Pacifics and Hudsons, these Atlantics continued to turn in admirable performances. During the acute motive power shortages of World War II, the E's proved their worth. ∎

(Top photo) One reason that No. 90 is assigned to the Strasburg's heavier trains can be seen in the photo opposite. Westbound trains stop at Groffs Grove where the ascending grade is 1.5%. Getting a seven or eight car train started requires a locomotive with considerable tractive effort. The 90 has just that, as well as drivers of sufficient size to comfortably accommodate the railroad's schedules. The Grove is also the location of the passing siding, where the hourly and half-hourly trains meet and pass one another. This scene shows the two trains passing.

(Second photo) In this photo, No. 90, taken in early 1983, is sporting its new tender lettering, as engineer Ervin White gets his seven car train rolling up the long 1.2% grade between Cherry Hill and Esbenshade crossing. The black smoke indicates that the fireman is busy with the coal scoop. On the westbound trip, the fireman shovels nearly half a ton of coal into the hungry firebox of No. 90.

(Third photo) Eastbound, Strasburg motive power normally backs. In this rare photo taken March 18, 1973, Strasburg's No. 89 is running forward eastbound. The Strasburg has no facilities for turning cars or locomotives, so it must wait until the turntable at the Railroad Museum Of Pennsylvania across the street is available. The 89 was turned shortly after this photo was taken. In the world of railroading, where practicable, it is desirable to have all motive power facing the same direction in order to simplify communications between the train crew and enginemen.

(Bottom photo) In the lower photo Linn Moedinger is shown atop No. 89 after flood waters of the Susquehanna River had subsided. He is indicating how high the water had been during the peak of the flood. To the left in the picture is the firehouse to which he retreated when railroad officials ordered everyone out of the yards. Most freight cars in Buttonwood yards were tossed about like matchsticks, but the 89's weight kept it on the rails.

ALL PHOTOGRAPHS – William Moedinger

The Strasburg's stable of immaculately groomed steam locomotives is matched with a meticulously maintained fleet of passenger coaches, enabling the railroad to provide up to two complete trains for off-line events and functions in which an old-time steam train is crucial to the theme of the celebration. Strasburg steam trains have been used over the years in many motion pictures and TV commercials. In the photo above, a Strasburg train is shown nearing its destination on the morning of November 19, 1988, as it portrays the train Abraham Lincoln rode over the same railroad between Hanover and Gettysburg 125 years earlier enroute to his famous Gettysburg address. Sponsored by the Battle of Gettysburg 125th Anniversary Commission, it carried a great many members of the PA. Senate and the PA. House of Representatives, as well as United States Supreme Court Chief Justice William Rehnquist who was the featured speaker at the re-enactment of this historic event at the National Cemetery later in the day.

LOCOMOTIVE 475

Locomotive 475 was built in June 1906 by Burnham, Williams & Co. (Baldwin Locomotive Works) for the Norfolk & Western Railway. Known as a twelve-wheel type because of its 4-8-0 wheel arrangement, it was a large locomotive in its day, built to pull heavy main line coal trains that comprised the bulk of Norfolk & Western freight traffic at that time.

As trains grew longer and locomotives became larger, the 475 was gradually downgraded to branch line, mixed train service. During its fifty-year life, the 475 performed well, but the coming of the diesel locomotive saw it retired in 1956 and moved to N & W's Schaffers Crossing yards where she became the roundhouse pet, operating occasionally to power excursions or to perform at historical functions. The 475 was finally sold for scrap to the Virginia Scrap Iron and Metal company where it narrowly escaped the dismantler's torch when William C. Armagost purchased it and removed it to a siding at Holsopple, PA. Mr. Armagost took steps to preserve the engine and covered it with a tarp. It remained here until May of 1980 when it was purchased by Mr. H. Stuart Kuyper who had it shipped to the Illinois Railway Museum where it was to have undergone repairs.

ALL PHOTOGRAPHS – William Moedinger

Unfortunately, while the 475 was in transit to the Illinois Railway Museum, Mr. Kuyper died and it was left to the Pella Historical Society. The historical society, it seems, was not interested in the locomotive and sold it to Mr. Kuyper's two daughters. The daughters subsequently donated the locomotive to the Boone Railroad Historical Society, operators of the Boone and Scenic Valley Railroad. From 1985 until June, 1991, the 475 was stored on a siding in Boone, Iowa.

Early in 1991, the Strasburg Rail Road offered the Boone and Scenic Railroad $100,000 for the 475. The offer was accepted, and in late June three shop people and the president flew to Boone to prepare the locomotive for the trip to Strasburg. Engine and tender were partially dismantled and loaded on three Trailer Train flat cars for the journey. On Saturday, July 20, 1991, the three flat cars arrived at Leaman Place Junction shortly after midnight. The final leg of the journey, between Dillerville and Leaman Place Junction, over Amtrak's electrified division, had to be made after the last suburban electric train made its last trip of the day so that the power could be cut off.

The 475's stack, according to Amtrak, was too close to the overhead trolley wire.

In the course of the ensuing 27 months in Strasburg shops, the 475 underwent a complete restoration in order to erase the effects of six years unprotected exposure to the weather. In addition to the $100,000 paid for the locomotive, rigging and transporting the locomotive and tender cost $32,974, and restoration in Strasburg shops cost another $508,460, bringing the total cost of transforming a rusty derelict into an operable steam locomotive to $641,434. ∎

PARADISE TOWNSHIP
William Moedinger

America's oldest short line railroad penetrates an arcadian wonderland, a land of rare bucolic charm reminiscent of pleasanter yesterdays when the entire nation was agriculturally oriented. In their ride on the ancient Strasburg, passengers experience the simple pleasures of an age that relished the going with as much fervor as the getting there. Between terminals and away from crowded highways, they relive an age innocent of air-conditioning and free from the curse of sealed windows when the traveler could fill his lungs with the fragrance of the countryside. Here, with coach windows raised to their fullest, or from seats in one of the two open coaches carried on each train during clement weather, passengers soon learn that the going can still be fun on the Strasburg Rail Road.

William Moedinger

THE TIME MACHINE

The linking of separate geographic places is generally conceded to be the principal function of a railroad. Over the years, however, and particularly since 1958, the primary function of the Strasburg Rail Road has largely given way to a secondary function that has not only brought renewed vigor and vitality to the aged carrier but also fame of considerable magnitude. The linking of separate times has become its foremost preoccupation. To take passage aboard its ancient coaches is akin to turning back the hands of time to the turn of the century.

Not only are its locomotives, cars and structures the real thing (some dating back into the 80's); but the country through which it operates is predominantly rural and farmed by a people who haven't significantly changed their methods of farming during the past three-quarters of a century. While the railroad is not paralleled by highway, the four roads which it crosses at grade between terminals are trafficked by the horse and buggy. Between these roads, the Strasburg's right of way is flanked on both sides by prosperous, small family farms of the type that have already disappeared from many rural sections of our country. The majority of these farms now belong to the Amish who still rely entirely on animal power and the forces of nature, such as wind and water, to perform many of the functions around the farm. The sight of these people tilling the soil is a familiar one from the railroad's turn-of-the-century coaches.

Here, within forty miles of megalopolis, is the turn of the century in microcosm. ■

The four roads which cross Strasburg Rail Road tracks are used heavily by the neighboring Amish farmers, particularly on Sunday mornings and late afternoons when these religious folks are on their ways to and from the various home church services. In the upper photo, an Amish lad with a courting buggy is on his way to pick a lady friend on a warm spring afternoon. In the lower photo, a married couple paused at the Cherry Hill crossing to allow the train to pass on a chilly December afternoon. They have spent all day at church services in a neighbor's farm and are now on their way home to take care of the chore of milking, which must be done morning and night, three hundred and sixty-five days a year.

Gordon Roth

William Moedinger

The Amish horse and buggy is a familiar sight from Strasburg coach windows. In the top photo, one waits at a farmer's crossing for the train to pass. The middle photo shows Amish lads lined up along the highway at the railroad's East Strasburg terminal. Since the opening of the Railroad Museum of Pennsylvania across the highway, traffic congestion has forced the lads away from this location; but prior to that these boys showed up here every weekend to offer tourists an opportunity to ride behind real horsepower. In the bottom photo, an Amish lad is given a disapproving glance from his elders in the passing buggy. Commercializing the Sabbath is held in low esteem by the highly religious Amish folks.

ALL PHOTOGRAPHS – William Moedinger

PENNSYLVANIA SPECIAL
William Moedinger

On June 9, 1982, the Strasburg Rail Road Company celebrated its 150th birthday by running two special trains: one departing East Strasburg at 6 PM, the other at 7 PM. From the tip of the pilot to the marker lights on the last coach, the consist was pure Pennsylvania Railroad. Glistening under the early evening sun from the spit-and-polish grooming, 4-4-0 No. 1223 provided the muscle. Behind 1223's tender, equally groomed for the occasion, were four priceless pieces of passenger rolling stock from the ornate pre-steel era around the turn of the century, consisting of express-baggage No. 6076, passenger baggage combine No. 4639. Deluxe vestibule coach No. 8177 and open platform coach No. 3556. In the above photo, the 6 PM section is shown scorching the ballast as it approaches Paradise Lane westbound. With his left hand on the throttle, engineer Linn Moedinger wears his black derby for the occasion. Standing on the deck immediately behind the engineer, taking a breather after a long session with the coal scoop on the long pull to Esbenshade's Crossing, is fireman Stephen Weaver. The Pennsylvania Railroad's famous Pennsylvania special rides the rails again!

William Moedinger

150TH BIRTHDAY

When a railroad has been in business under the same name for one hundred and fifty years, a celebration is in order. On June 9, 1982, the Strasburg Rail Road Company reached the century and one half mark. And celebrate the railroad did. With festivities that involved employees, officers, stockholders and the general public, the celebration lasted for nine days, embracing the two weekends on either side of the actual birth date.

In the course of those nine days, twenty-three special trains were operated by the railroad. Three trains comprised of No. 1, the Plymouth locomotive and a single coach were operated exclusively for the benefit of the road's 180 stockholders as a re-creation of the little one-car trains that enabled the railroad to re-enter the passenger business back in 1959. Two special all Pennsy steam trains were operated on the Wednesday

evening of the Strasburg's birthday in connection with ceremonies at the Railroad Museum Of Pennsylvania for the benefit of visiting dignitaries. And, on the Saturdays and Sundays immediately preceding and following the Strasburg's birthday, a total of eighteen special, all Pennsy steam trains were scheduled for the benefit of the general public.

On the page opposite, as well as the two following pages, are pictures of these trains. The running of these twenty all-Pennsy steam trains was not only a way for the Strasburg to celebrate a prestigious birthday, but also an opportunity to salute fond memories of the Pennsylvania Railroad through whose kind offices the little railroad managed to survive during the more than one hundred and ten years that the two railroads interchanged freight at Leaman Place. ∎

During the nine days that the Strasburg operated the all Pennsy steam train, the public had an opportunity to ride what may very well be the oldest train in the world. The average age of locomotive 1223 and the four wooden coaches in 1982 was 85 years. Every one of the four cars was built before the present century. Above, the eastbound special approaches Cherry Hill. In the lower photo, the westbound special approaches Carpenters Crossing. The two center photos identify the special on the front and rear of the train. That last coach, incidentally, had reached its 97th birthday in 1982.

ALL PHOTOGRAPHS – William Moedinger

The running of the three special trains consisting of No. 1 and one open-platform coach for the exclusive benefit of the Strasburg's stockholders brought back fond memories to some of those who had been around that January Sunday afternoon in 1959 when the railroad re-entered the passenger business with the identical locomotive and a lone passenger coach. No one dreamed, back on that cold Sunday afternoon, that those two one-car trains were the beginning of a passenger business that would account for nearly six million revenue riders during the ensuing twenty-three years. The four photos on this page show the Strasburg Rail Road stockholders special on Saturday, June 5, 1982. As the photos suggest, it was a wet, overcast day; but virtually every stockholder within driving distance turned out for an opportunity to experience railroading on their railroad as it had been a quarter of a century earlier. The above photo shows the train approaching Paradise Lane crossing. Second photo from the top depicts the Plymouth running around the lone coach at Leaman Place. The third photo shows a later section backing into the clear so that the regular train could run around its train. Umbrellas were the order of the day. In the lower photo, Vice-president and chief Engineer Winston Gottschalk, one of the original stockholders who purchased the railroad in 1958, reflects on the improvements made to the Strasburg over the past twenty-three years.

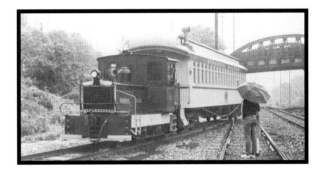

ALL PHOTOGRAPHS – William Moedinger

TRAIN TI
William Moedin

This towerman's view of train time at East Strasburg reveals at a glance why railroads built signal towers in order to expedite the movement of trains over heavily trafficked main lines, at junctions or wherever switches were needed to move trains from one track to another. Long before centralized traffic control or the age of electronics, towermen were the eyes and ears of the dispatcher. With an overall view of each train that passed his tower, the towerman reported not only the exact time it passed but any unusual circumstances, such as a hot box, for example, that he thought the dispatcher should know about. In response to orders from the dispatcher, towermen actually threw switches and changed the positions of signals through a system of huge levers and connecting rods. The only time these men left their lofty perch was when they had orders to hand up to a passing train. Inside the tower the constant clatter of the telegraph kept each man informed of the location and progress of each train on that particular division. For ninety-eight years, until it was moved to its present location, this tower protected train movements at the intersection of the Northern Central and Cumberland Valley Railroads on the west bank of the Susquehanna River at Lemoyne, Pa.

William Moedinger

"J" TOWER

"J" Tower, as it will be known when restoration is finally completed in the near future, was built in 1885 by the Cumberland Valley Railroad, using the prevailing Pennsylvania Railroad style of architecture. When Conrail withdrew the tower from service in 1983, after ninety-eight years of service, demolition seemed imminent. Ted Xaras, known widely for his railroad oriented art work and paintings, persuaded members of the Lancaster Chapter of The National Railway Historical Society that saving and restoring this tower should become the chapter's number one project. A classic example of Pennsylvania Railroad signal tower design of the period, it is of particular interest historically as well as architecturally in that it has both a bay window and a cupola.

The Lancaster Chapter accepted the challenge; and, galvanizing words into action, members approached the task with the usual dispatch and zeal. By Christmas of 1984, the tower had been dismantled, transported to Strasburg and reassembled on ground and a foundation provided by the Strasburg Rail Road Company. Restoration has been going on ever since. In addition to the work performed by private contractors, individual members, under the direction of member Ken Murry, have contributed a great deal of expertise and time to the project. When completed, the tower is expected to be open to the public so it may see how the trains were kept running when the business of railroading was in its prime. ■

AN ALBUM OF COUNTRY RAILROADING

ALL PHOTOGRAPHS – William Moedi

People from all walks of life have discovered that the nine-mile round trip over America's oldest shortline railroad is a veritable excursion into history. At the top of page 36, a mid-afternoon westbound train approaches the railroad's picnic grove. The lower photo on page 36 shows another westbound train passing Carpenters station. At the top of this page the photographer stood on the top of Cherry Hill as an eastbound train crosses the highway of the same name. At the bottom of this page, with the Strasburg's newest locomotive on point, a mid-afternoon westbound train climbs the grade between Cherry Hill and the Esbenshade Turkey Farm. Almost within the very shadow of megalopolis, the ancient Strasburg Rail Road traverses a land of thrifty farms and homesteads of gentlefolk who observe a way of life rarely encountered anywhere today.

ALL PHOTOGRAPHS – William Moedinger

Before the era of paved highways and internal combustion, parks and picnic groves were fairly common along branch lines and the numerous short lines of the day. Often located in heavily wooded areas sufficiently remote

from urban centers, they generated many fares for those railroads serving them. In an effort to recreate the typical short line of that era, the Strasburg Rail Road developed Groff's Grove into a free picnic spot midway between East Strasburg and Paradise. Named for John Groff, owner of the farm on which the grove is located, Groffs Grove offers patrons of the railroad a relaxing spot to hold a family picnic away from the hustle and bustle of everyday life. The grove is also the location of the railroad's passing siding which permits trains going in opposite directions to pass one another. In the above photo, No. 90, with the up train, waits for the passing of No. 1223 and its train. In the

lower photo, No. 7002, the latest addition to the Strasburg roster of iron horses, arrives at the grove with the up train. But a railroad is a great deal more than engines, coaches and tracks. A railroad is people, knowledgeable in their profession and dedicated to serving and pleasing those who patronize it. Two who happened to be handy when the author was there with his camera were conductors Bill Marks and Bill Kipphorn. In the left photo, microphone in hand, conductor Marks is asking his passengers to observe certain safety precautions during the ride. Just above in the right photo, conductor Kipphorn has his arm raised as he performs the time-honored ritual of the brake test, which, in the interests of safety, is done whenever a locomotive is coupled to the train.

ALL PHOTOGRAPHS – William Moedinger

Maintaining and operating an aged fleet of steam locomotives requires a force of competent, resourceful shop men. Above left is Glen Lefever putting the finishing touches on the cab of the 7002. Above right is Vice-President and chief mechanical officer Linn Moedinger checking the performance of the air pump. Getting trains over the road also requires the skills of an engine crew: an engineer who knows how to conserve steam and a fireman who knows how to make steam. To the right, as seen from the "J" tower, the fireman takes a breather and wipes the sweat from his brow after a twenty-minute hassle with the coal scoop. Getting a nine-car train up the hill from Paradise requires that he shovel one quarter ton of coal into a roaring fire through a small fire door that never seems to hold still. In the lower photo, the half hour train commences the long pull from the Cherry Hill station to the Esbenshade Road crossing.

ALL PHOTOGRAPHS – William Moedinger

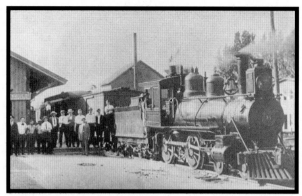

From the Collection of William Moedinger

William Moedinger

William Moedinger

When the train whistles for Carpenters crossing and there seems to be an echo after each blast, our conductors tell folks it's the whistle of a ghost railroad on the other side of the hill. Some folks are inclined to take this explanation with a grain of salt. However, their story is not a complete fabrication. Just four miles southwest from the crossing, as the crow flies, there was, indeed, a little narrow gauge railroad that ran from Quarryville to Oxford. In the top photo, that little three-foot gauge train is shown just about to depart the Quarryville station on its very last run on April 14, 1917.

On Thursday, June 9, 1983, the Newcomen Society Of The United States celebrated its sixtieth birthday by honoring the Strasburg Rail Road on the completion of its sesquicentennial year with a dinner in the main exhibition hall of the Railroad Museum Of Pennsylvania. Prior to the dinner, as its contribution to this gala occasion, a reception was held aboard a special train provided by the railroad. That train is shown in the middle photo westbound coming off Long Curve double-headed with engines 1223 and 90.

Some folks are surprised to learn that the Strasburg Rail Road hauls freight. Actually, when the present stockholders purchased the railroad back in 1958, they planned to restore the railroad with freight revenues developed by the carload business received in interchange with the Pennsylvania railroad. In a very few months, the new owners realized that the railroad could not survive on the meager freight income alone and that the future of the railroad would have to depend on passenger revenues. There still is some freight business, however, and in the lower photo No. 90 hustles westbound with five heavily laden hoppers of plastic pellets which originated some 2,200 miles west of Leaman Place on Missouri Pacific's main line in western Texas.